What's in this book

This book belongs to

_____

T0351538

超人爸爸 Superdad

学习内容 Contents

沟通 Communication

向他人道早
Greet people in the morning

向他人打招呼
Greet people at any time of the day

向他人道别
Say goodbye to people

生词 New words

★ 早　　good morning

★ 你好　hello

★ 再见　goodbye

爸爸　father, dad

妈妈　mother, mum

浩浩　Hao Hao
浩浩（丁浩）是本系列丛书的主角。他是中国人，今年六岁，与爸爸、妈妈和姐姐同住在某英语国家，家里还有只小狗。

背景介绍：
晚上睡觉前，妈妈给浩浩讲了《超级英雄》的故事。

浩浩妈妈

浩浩

句式 Sentence patterns

爸爸，早！   Good morning, Dad!

浩浩，你好！   Hello, Hao Hao!

妈妈，再见！   Goodbye, Mum!

跨学科学习 Project

制作手偶，问候他人
Make a hand puppet and say
hello and goodbye

文化 Cultures

中国人打招呼的方式
Chinese ways of greetings

参考答案：
1 I listen to music/watch TV/read a storybook.
2 *The Superhero.*
3 Yes, he does.

Get ready

1 What do you do before you go to sleep?

2 What story is Mum reading to Hao Hao?

3 Does Hao Hao like the story?

浩浩爸爸

小狗名叫布朗尼
(Brownie)，是一只
小猎犬 (beagle)。

zǎo
早!

早上第一次见面时，可以跟别人
互相说："早!"

故事大意：
浩浩梦见自己上学快迟到了，爸爸竟然变身超人送他到学校。
(老师通过参考问题引导学生逐步了解情节发展，最后揭开
故事的悬念。)

爸爸，早! 妈妈，早!

参考问题和答案：

1 Who can you see? (I can see Hao Hao, his dad and mum.)

2 What time of the day is it? (It is the morning.)

3 How does Hao Hao greet his parents in the morning? ('Good morning!')

4 Why do you think Hao Hao is in a hurry? (Because he got up late and is now going to be late for school.)

浩浩，再见！

参考问题和答案：

1 What happened? (Hao Hao missed the school bus.)

2 How does Hao Hao look? (He looks worried.)

3 What are Hao Hao's schoolmates saying to him? ('Goodbye!')

见面打招呼时，可以跟别人互相说："你好！"

超人，你好！

参考问题和答案：

1 Who is the tall man? (He is Hao Hao's dad.)

2 Does Hao Hao recognize the tall man? (No, he does not.)

3 How does Hao Hao greet the tall man? ('Hello!')

你好！ 爸爸送我上学。

参考问题和答案：

1 Does Hao Hao know who the tall man is now? (Yes, he does.)
2 Who is Hao Hao talking to? (A bird.)
3 Where are they flying to? (Hao Hao's school.)

谢谢爸爸。再见！

参考问题和答案：

1 What time is it now? (It is eight o'clock.)

2 Is Hao Hao late for school? (No, he is not. He has arrived on time.)

3 Hao Hao is waving goodbye to Dad. What do you think he is saying? ('Goodbye!')

延伸活动：
学生分组进行角色扮演并续编故事及在续编故事中运用"早！""你好！"和"再见！"三句话。

浩浩，早。上学了。

参考问题和答案：

1   Why is Hao Hao still in bed? (Because what just happened was a dream.)
2   How do we know Hao Hao is dreaming? (You can see the cloud bubbles.)
3   What time is it now? (It is seven o'clock.)
4   Why is Mum waking up Hao Hao? (Because it is time for school.)

Let's think

1 How does Hao Hao usually go to school? Trace the correct line.

提醒学生观察第5页的图。

参考方式:

坐小汽车、坐地铁、坐的士、坐飞机、坐火箭……(学生画完后小组互相交流,看看谁的方式最快、谁的方式最有趣。)

2 Can you think of other ways to send Hao Hao to school? Draw below.

New words

1 Learn the new words.

早！

妈妈

爸爸

再见！

你好！

浩浩

早上见面打招呼时，用"早"或"你好"都可以。

玲玲（丁玲），浩浩的姐姐

2 Match the words to the pictures. Write the letters.

a 早　　　　b 再见　　　　c 你好

b

a

c

提醒学生，图1是夕阳落山，图2是太阳初升，图3是月亮当空，在跟星星打招呼。

听听说说 Listen and say

 1 Look, listen and repeat.

1

2

3

2 Look at the pictures. Listen to the st...

浩浩，早。上学了！

妈妈，早！

浩浩，早！

早，妈妈送我
上学！

参考问题和答案：
1 How do you say 'to go to school' in Chinese? (It is 上学.)
2 Do you wish that you could fly? Why or why not? (Yes, I do...
Because I would be able to go anywhere I want if I could fly...
No, I do not. Because I am afraid of heights.)

第三题录音稿：
1 浩浩，你好！
2 浩浩，早！
3 浩浩，再见！

d say.

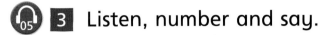 3 Listen, number and say.

Task

Speak Chinese to your friends. Write their names and tick when you have done so.

提醒学生将朋友的名字写在这一列的空格内。	早！	你好！	再见！
Hao Hao	✓	✓	✓
1			
2			
3			

Game

游戏方法：
学生听老师说句子，并指向相应的石头，指错的话就会掉进水里，不能过到水池对岸。
参考路径："妈妈，早！""爸爸，早！""你好！""早！""再见！"

Listen to your teacher. Find the way out of the crocodile pond.

Song

🎧 06 **Listen and sing.**

"早"和"早上好"都可用于早上见面打招呼。

早上好，早上好，

爸爸妈妈早上好！

我去上学说再见，

爸爸妈妈说再见！

课堂用语 Classroom language

看
look

听
listen

说
say

读
read

写
write

画
draw

写一写 Write

笔画记忆方法：

1 笔画结合实物图有助记忆。

2 老师示范笔画功夫，学生跟着做："横"是两个手臂左右伸直，"竖"是两个手臂向上伸直举高，手掌相对，双脚站直并拢。

1 Learn and trace the strokes.

Strokes（笔画）是构成汉字字形的最小连笔单位，可具体分为横、竖、撇、点、折等等。

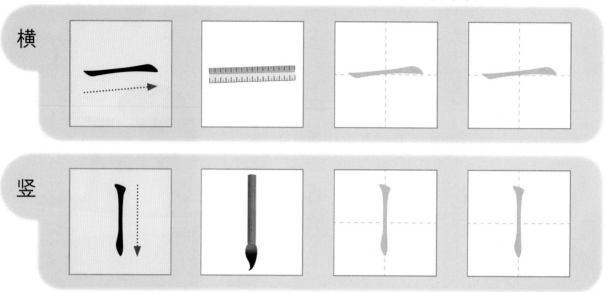

2 Learn the component. Circle 日 in the characters.

Components（部件）由笔画组成，是具有组配汉字功能的构字单位。

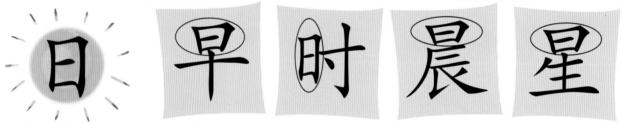

引导学生观察图画并猜测部件含义，说明同一部件在不同汉字里形状可能不太一样。

3 Colour the suns and draw arrows to shoot down two of them.

后羿射日：中国古代神话，善于射箭的后羿将天空中的十个骄阳射下九个，拯救了黎民。

4 Trace and write the character.

Characters（汉字）是汉语书写的最基本单元。一个汉字对一个拼音音节。

早	早	早

提醒学生先按笔顺指引用手指在空中写两次目标生字，再在田字格内描摹和书写。

提醒学生"早"字的书写顺序为从上到下。可结合"汉字小常识"告诉他们上下结构的汉字的书写顺序都是从上到下。

5 Write and say.

问问学生太阳和公鸡在早上见面时怎样互相打招呼。

汉字小常识 Did you know?

Some characters are made up of upper and lower components.

Colour the upper component red and the lower component green.

该结构中的上下部件所占比例不一定相同。如："早"字上小下大，"爸"字大概五五分。

Cultures

1 ## Do you know how Chinese people greet each other?

中国古代同辈人见面行礼时通常双手合握于胸前，男子右手握拳，左手在外，女子则相反。

In old China, people greeted each other in this way.

Now, Chinese adults shake hands when they meet.

Children usually wave their hands.

延伸活动：

学生先角色扮演中国人打招呼的方式，再讨论其他国家的打招呼礼仪，最后轮流在全班面前表演。（如：毛利人互相碰鼻子来打招呼；意大利人通常快速亲吻彼此的脸颊，先右侧，再左侧。）

2 **How do you greet people? Draw on the right.**

你好!

你好!

材料：一把剪刀、一支水笔、一根雪糕棍、两根彩色扭扭棒。

1 Make an ice lolly hand puppet.

①

② 从一根扭扭棒上剪取两段同样长短的线段，缠绕在雪糕棍顶端。

从另一根扭扭棒上剪取一段适当长度的线段，缠绕在雪糕棍中间。

Be careful with the scissors!

③

④ 用水笔为雪糕棍画笑脸。

⑤

2 Say hello and goodbye to your friends.

……

你好！

再见！

早！

学生拿着做好的雪糕棍人偶在教室内互相走动问候，并看看谁的人偶做得最可爱。

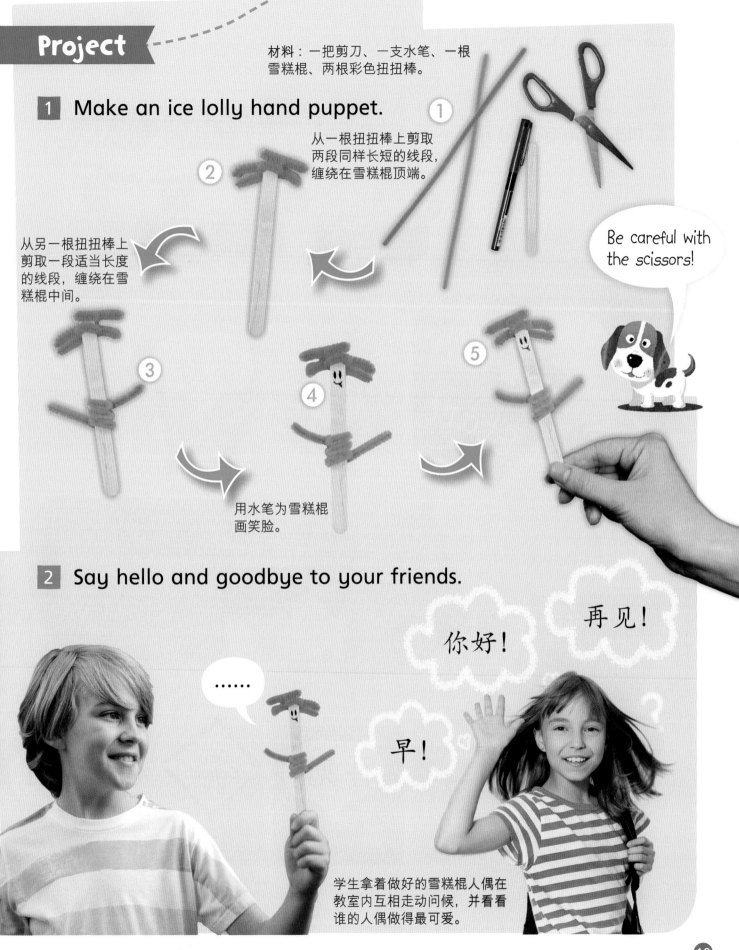

1 Play the board game.

评核方法：
学生两人一组，互相考察评核表内单词和句子的听说读写。交际沟通部分由老师朗读要求，学生再互相对话。如果达到了某项技能要求，则用色笔将星星或小辣椒涂色。

2 **Work with your friend. Colour the stars and the chillies.**

Words and sentences	说	读	写
早	☆	☆	☆
你好	☆	☆	🌶
再见	☆	☆	🌶
爸爸，早！	☆	🌶	🌶
妈妈，再见！	☆	🌶	🌶
浩浩，你好！	☆	🌶	🌶

Greet people in the morning	☆
Greet people at any time of the day	☆
Say goodbye to people	☆

3 **What does your teacher say?**

评核建议：
根据学生课堂表现，分别给予"太棒了！(Excellent!)""不错！(Good!)"或"继续努力！(Work harder!)"的评价，再让学生圈出左侧对应的表情，以记录自己的学习情况。

My teacher says ...

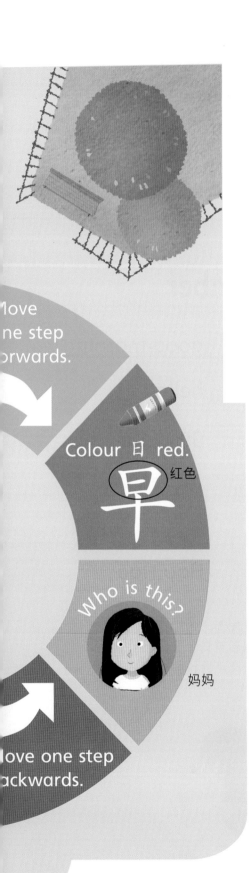

Move one step forwards.

Colour 早 red.
红色
早

Who is this?

妈妈

Move one step backwards.

分享 Sharing

Words I remember

早	zǎo	good morning
你好	nǐ hǎo	hello
再见	zài jiàn	goodbye
爸爸	bà ba	father, dad
妈妈	mā ma	mother, mum
浩浩	hào hao	Hao Hao

延伸活动：
1 学生用手遮盖英文，读中文单词，并思考单词意思；
2 学生用手遮盖中文单词，看着英文说出对应的中文单词；
3 学生两人一组，尽量运用中文单词分角色复述故事。

Other words

超人	chāo rén	superman
送	sòng	to take
我	wǒ	I, me
上学	shàng xué	to go to school
谢谢	xiè xie	thanks

School bus

OXFORD
UNIVERSITY PRESS

Oxford University Press is a department of the University of Oxford.
It furthers the University's objective of excellence in research, scholarship,
and education by publishing worldwide. Oxford is a registered trade mark of
Oxford University Press in the UK and in certain other countries

Published in Hong Kong by
Oxford University Press (China) Limited
39th Floor, One Kowloon, 1 Wang Yuen Street, Kowloon Bay,
Hong Kong

Illustrated by Anne Lee and Wildman

Photographs for reproduction permitted by Dreamstime.com

China National Publications Import & Export (Group) Corporation is an authorized distributor of
Oxford Elementary Chinese.

Please contact content@cnpiec.com.cn or 86-10-65856782

ISBN: 978-0-19-942968-4

10 9 8 7 6 5 4 3 2

Teacher's Edition
ISBN: 978-0-19-082147-0

10 9 8 7 6 5 4 3 2